Wuthering Heights
by Emily Brontë

A Study Guide by Ray Moore

Acknowledgements:
To all my students through the years who taught me so much about this book. Special thanks to my wife Barbara for preparing the text for publication

Picture:

Emily Brontë, in a painting by her brother Branwell Brontë. This image is in the public domain; its copyright has expired.

Contents

Wuthering Heights by Emily Brontë

Dramatis Personnæ - Meet the characters

The Earnshaw Family:

Mr. Earnshaw - A loving father and a good, compassionate man.

Mrs. Earnshaw - His wife who dies shortly after the arrival of Heathcliff.

Catherine Earnshaw - despite her love for Heathcliff, she will marry Edgar Linton because he can offer her wealth and social status.

Hindley Earnshaw - Catherine's brother - his dislike of Heathcliff eats away at him and he ends his life in drunken dissipation.

Frances Earnshaw - wife of Hindley who dies shortly after the birth of her son.

Hareton Earnshaw - son of Hindley and Frances - on his father's death, Heathcliff treats him as a servant in revenge for the manner in which Hindley treated him.

Heathcliff - a Liverpool orphan boy who is adopted by Mr. Earnshaw - he is immediately resented by Hindley, but as they grow up he and Catherine fall deeply in love - he marries Isabella Linton as part of his plan to gain revenge against the Lintons.

Linton Heathcliff - son of Heathcliff and Isabella, he is brought up in London by his mother - he is a weak and sickly boy - Heathcliff forces him to marry Catherine Linton, but he dies soon afterwards.

Earnshaw Servants:

Ellen (Nelly) Dean - Catherine's servant at Wuthering Heights - she is the main narrator of the story.

Joseph - an elderly servant at Wuthering Heights - he is a religious bigot and a cruel man.

Zila - housekeeper at Wuthering Heights when Heathcliff is master there.

The Linton Family:

Mr. Linton - owner of Thrushcross Grange and therefore a member of the local gentry.

Mrs. Linton - a social snob who keeps Heathcliff away from her own children as much as she can.

Edgar Linton - a handsome but weak man who marries Catherine - he is no match for Heathcliff who gains power over him and his family in revenge for his marriage to Catherine.

Isabella Linton - Edgar's sister.

Catherine (Cathy) Linton - daughter of Edgar and Catherine Earnshaw who shares many character traits with her mother.

Mr. Green - Edgar Linton's lawyer.

Primary Narrator:

Mr. Lockwood - Heathcliff's tenant at Wuthering Heights who comes to the moors to find solitude.

Themes

Social Class:

Victorian society was strictly divided by class. Perhaps the most significant single division was between those who were and those who were not 'gentlemen.' A gentleman did not actually work for a living. His income came from ownership of land and from inherited wealth which was invested. The distinction was partly a matter of wealth, but it was much more a matter of birth: Heathcliff is born into the working class (or perhaps even worse into the vagrant class) and he can never become a gentleman.

Mr. Earnshaw is a reasonably prosperous farmer, but he is not a gentleman. One indication of this is that he does not own a carriage - the ultimate status symbol of the day. His daughter Catherine has a strong desire to improve her status and life-style by marriage and the obvious solution is to marry into the local gentry family.

Love:

If you have read *Pride and Prejudice* by Jane Austen you will know that in that novel romantic love and a socially advantageous marriage go hand-in-hand: Elizabeth sincerely loves Mr. Darcy, who just happens to be one of the richest men in England, when she marries him, and the same can be said of her sister Jane's feelings for Mr. Bingley. In this novel, however, romantic love (an altogether more passionate state than Jane Austen conceived it to be) is at odds with 'marrying up.' The result is that whilst Jane and Darcy live happily ever after, Catherine Earnshaw makes a life-destroying error in marrying Edgar Linton instead of the man she actually loves - the man she will always love, even beyond the grave.

Revenge:

The Elizabethan philosopher Francis Bacon wrote, "Revenge is a kind of wild justice; which, the more a man's nature runs to, the more ought law to weed it out." Heathcliff is motivated throughout by the desire for revenge which, not surprisingly eats away at him and finally destroys him. Initially, he hates the poverty into which he was born, but his hatred soon becomes focused on Hindley Earnshaw who resents the love which his father obviously has for the wild urchin he brings to Wuthering Heights and treats Heathcliff with cruel disdain. When Catherine Earnshaw marries Edgar Linton, Heathcliff's desire for revenge extends to the Linton family. All must suffer, the innocent as well as the guilty to appease his anger and hatred.

Wuthering Heights by Emily Brontë

Genre

Wuthering Heights is most frequently called a Gothic novel a genre of literature that combines elements of horror and romance. The first Gothic novel is usually taken to be Horace Walpole's *The Castle of Otranto* (1764); Jane Austen satirized the genre in *Northanger Abbey* (1803). "Prominent features of Gothic fiction include terror (both psychological and physical), mystery, the supernatural, ghosts, haunted houses and Gothic architecture, castles, darkness, death, decay, doubles, madness, secrets and hereditary curses" (Wikipedia).

The story of *Wuthering Heights* really begins with Lockwood's terrifying encounter at night with the ghost of Catherine Earnshaw still desperately seeking re-entry to her childhood home. The character of Heathcliff at times appears to be that of a malicious sprite rather than a human child. Above all, the extreme passionate nature of human love, which crosses the boundaries of social class and of life and death itself, marks this novel as owing much to the Gothic novel genre.

Setting

The action of the novel extends from the 1770s to 1802. The setting is the Yorkshire Moors, whose beauty is matched only by the harshness of its climate. The bleak farmhouse of Wuthering Heights and the more sheltered and refined Thrushcross Grange stand in opposition, the former representing the world of nature and the latter the world of man, manners and culture.

How to use this study guide:

The questions are not designed to test you but to help you to locate and to understand characters, settings, and themes in the text. They do not normally have simple answers, nor is there always one answer. Consider a range of possibly interpretations - preferably by discussing the questions with others.

Literary terms are in **bold underlined.** These terms are defined towards the end of this guide. An activity is also included to aid in the understanding of these terms.

Study Guide Questions

Chapter One

1. The **frame narrative** ['nothing in the book is written from the **perspective** of an unbiased **narrator**' (Phillips and Bourneuf)]:
   a) Why has Lockwood come to live at Thrushcross Grange? (What did his mother mean when she said that he would 'never have a comfortable home'? What incident the previous summer appears to have motivated Lockwood's move? When you have read the whole novel, reflect on the way in which the themes of the **narrative** in which Lockwood becomes involved relate to the incident from which he is seeking to escape.)
   b) Analyze Lockwood's explanations of his own temperament. (What does he say of his response to "showy displays of feelings"? How does he react to having gained a "reputation of deliberate heartlessness"? What indications are there that Lockwood is not so entirely antisocial as he imagines himself to be?)
   c) What is the basis for Lockwood's immediate attraction to Heathcliff whom he calls, "A capital fellow!"? How reliable does Lockwood appear to be as a **narrator**?
   d) Comment on the possible levels of meaning of the italicized words in Lockwood's description of Heathcliff as, "the *solitary* neighbor that I shall be *troubled* with."
2. Heathcliff:
   a) Give five details of Heathcliff's appearance, and explain how each detail gives the reader a clue to his temperament.
   b) Give five details of Heathcliff's behavior towards other characters and explain how each gives the reader a further clue to his temperament.
   c) What is the **paradox** that Lockwood notes when comparing Heathcliff's physical appearance with his "dress and manners"?
3. The **setting**:
   a) What relationship between Man and Nature is implied in the description of Wuthering Heights and the surrounding countryside?
   b) What features of the interior of Wuthering Heights are stressed? In what way is Heathcliff "a singular contrast to his abode and style of living"?

Wuthering Heights by Emily Brontë

Chapter Two

4. Hareton Earnshaw and Mrs. Heathcliff:
   a) What mistaken assumptions does Lockwood make about the relationship of Heathcliff, Hareton and Mrs. Heathcliff? What is their actual relationship?
   b) How does Hareton behave towards:
      * Lockwood?
      * Mrs.Heathcliff?
      * Heathcliff?
   c) How does Mrs. Heathcliff behave towards:
      * Hareton?
      * Joseph?
5. Lockwood's **frame narrative**:
   a) Lockwood makes use of **verbal irony** several times in his description of Mrs. Heathcliff. Give and analyze at least three examples. What is it about Mrs. Heathcliff that prompts Lockwood to use **irony**?
   b) What further evidence is there in this chapter that Lockwood's inability to read people and situations make him an unreliable **narrator**?
6. Heathcliff:
   a) What is it about Heathcliff's behavior in this chapter that leads Lockwood to conclude, "I no longer felt inclined to call Heathcliff a capital fellow"?
7. Zillah:
   What do we learn of this character?

Chapter Three

8. Lockwood's **frame narrative**:
   a) Into whose room is Lockwood taken by Zillah? What is peculiar about the construction of the bed in the room?
   b) From Catherine's diaries, what do you learn about the people who lived at Wuthering Heights at the time the diaries were written and of their relationship to one another? Who has recently died?
   c) What is the significance of Lockwood's first nightmare?
   d) How does Brontë make the appearance of Catherine **ambiguous**?
   e) Comment on the action by which Lockwood seeks to free his hand from Catherine's grasp? Does it surprise you?
   f) Analyze the **imagery** which Lockwood uses to describe his journey back to Thrushcross Grange ("My landlord... from Wuthering Heights.").
   g) Comment on the **tone** of Lockwood's account of his return to the Grange ("My human... my refreshment.").

9. Catherine:
   a) The name Catherine Earnshaw is scratched onto the pane a good many times "here and there varied to Catherine Heathcliff, and then again to Catherine Linton." Speculate on the writer's reasons for etching her name thus.
   b) Explain Lockwood's comment that Catherine's books were "well used, though not altogether for a legitimate purpose."
   c) What indications are given in the diaries of:
      • Catherine's rebellious nature?
      • Her relationship with Heathcliff?
   d) What do you think is the significance of the 'ghost' in Lockwood's second nightmare replying to his question about her identity with the words "Catherine Linton"?
   e) What explanation can you suggest for Catherine's claim, "'It is twenty years… I've been a waif for twenty years'"?
10. Heathcliff:
   a) Analyze Heathcliff's reaction when Lockwood tells him about the apparition at the window.
   b) What more do we learn about the relationship of Heathcliff and Mrs. Heathcliff?

Chapters Four and Five

11. How would you describe Lockwood's **mood** at the start of Chapter 4? How is this conveyed by the writer's use of language in the first paragraph?
12. In Mrs. Dean's **narrative**, what aspects of Heathcliff's appearance and character seem to support Mr. Earnshaw's statement that it is "'almost as if it [he]came from the devil'"?
13. How would you describe Mrs. Dean's feeling towards Cathy? Support your answer by reference to particular words and phrases which she uses to describe the young girl's behavior.

Chapter Six

14. Mrs. Dean calls Cathy and Heathcliff "as rude as savages" (a **simile**) and "the unfriended creatures" (a very original adjective). Comment on the significance of **diction** in these phrases.
15. There is considerable **foreshadowing** in this chapter. Comment in particular on:

- Heathcliff's statement, "'I'd not exchange for a thousand lives, my condition here, for Edgar Linton's at Thrushcross Grange.'" [Clue: And how might Cathy feel?]
- Mr. Linton's question, "'the villain [Heathcliff] scowls so plainly in his face; would it not be a kindness to the country to hang him at once, before he shows his nature in acts...?'"
- Mrs. Dean's prediction, "'There will more come of this business than you reckon on.'"

16. Contrast the initial description of the interior of Thrushcross Grange with the descriptions of Wuthering Heights at the same period.

Chapter Seven

17. What is the significance of Mrs. Dean's comment that, on her return to Wuthering Heights, Cathy appeared "instead of a wild, hatless little savage ... [like] a very dignified person"?
18. How does Cathy attempt to deal with the dilemma in which she finds herself because of the conflict between her loyalty to (and love of) Heathcliff and her attraction to the sophisticated world of the Lintons?
19. Contrast Heathcliff and Edgar Linton.
20. Lockwood tells Mrs. Dean, "'I could fancy a love for life here almost possible.'" What do you thing it is about the story that he has heard that has had such a profound effect on Lockwood?

Chapter Eight

21. Mrs. Dean reports that at this time Cathy adopts "a double character without exactly intending to deceive anyone." Explain what she means.
22. Mrs. Dean says of Heathcliff "he contrived to convey an impression of inward and outward repulsiveness." Comment on the significance of Brontë's use of the word "confused."
23. With detailed reference to the description of Edgar Linton's portrait, illustrate Mrs. Dean's **analogy**: "The contrast [between Edgar and Heathcliff] resembled what you see in exchanging a bleak, hilly, coal country for a beautiful fertile valley."

Chapter Nine

24. Explain Mrs. Dean's comment that Heathcliff's countenance "expressed... the intense anguish at having made himself the instrument of thwarting his own revenge."

25. Since Cathy gives Mrs. Dean plenty of reasons for her decision to marry Edgar, explain clearly her statement, "'In my soul and in my heart, I'm convinced I'm wrong.'" [Comment in detail on Cathy's **similes**, "'My love for Linton is like the foliage in the woods: time will change it, I'm well aware, as winter changes the trees. My love for Heathcliff resembles the eternal rocks beneath: a source of little visible delight, but necessary.'"]

26. Examine the **symbolism** of natural events in the description of Heathcliff's departure from Wuthering Heights. Would you agree with the criticism that the second half of this chapter is **melodramatic**? Justify your answer.

Chapter Ten

27. What is the significance of the writer's use of *verb tenses* in the **frame narrative** of the first two paragraphs?

28. Comment on the **symbolism** of Mrs. Dean's description of the view that Cathy and Edgar see through the open door of the Grange ("He lifted... wishes to see you, ma'am.'").

29. Cathy says of Edgar and Isabella, "'they are spoiled children.'" How does this comment relate to Mrs. Dean's description of Heathcliff and Edgar ("I descended... chose to speak.")?

30. When Cathy learns of Isabella's love for Heathcliff, she describes him in very negative terms. Speculate on what **motivates** Cathy.

31. What is Joseph suggesting about Heathcliff's motives for "befriending" Hindley in the speech which culminates with the **metaphor** "'her father's son gallops down t'broad road, while he [Heathcliff] flees afore to open t'pikes'"?

32. What is **foreshadowed** in Mrs. Dean's observation of Heathcliff's "grin" near the end of the chapter?

Chapter Eleven

33. In the first six pages of the chapter, the writer frequently uses **diction** which associated Heathcliff with the devil. Collect some examples.

34. Explain exactly what Heathcliff means when he says to Cathy, "'Having leveled my palace, don't erect a hovel and complacently admire your own charity in giving me that for a home.'"

35. What plan does Cathy share with Mrs. Dean whose object is to "break their hearts, by breaking my own"? Why does Nelly not take Cathy's resolution seriously?

Chapter Twelve

36. Several of the things that Cathy says in her delirium explain the ghostly apparition encountered by Lockwood in Chapter Three. An example is Cathy's exclamation, "'Oh, if I were but in my own bed in the old house!'" Find and explain other examples.
37. Analyze the **symbolism** of Thrushcross Grange, Wuthering Heights and the heather-covered hillsides with particular reference to the paragraph in which Cathy laments "'Why am I so changed?'"
38. Suggest an explanation for the attempt to hang Isabella's springer, Fanny.

Chapter Thirteen

39. In her letter, Isabella asks Nelly "Is Mr. Heathcliff a man? ...is he a devil?" Collect together short quotations from this chapter which suggest that the latter is true.
40. What do we learn from the letter of the state of affairs between Heathcliff and Hindley? [Put simply: Who owns Wuthering Heights?]

Chapter Fourteen

41. Heathcliff reports that on the night Isabella ran away with him, "'the first words I uttered were a wish that I had the hanging of every being belonging to her: possibly she took that exception for herself.'" Explain what you think Heathcliff actually meant.
42. Heathcliff says of Edgar's attempts to nurse Cathy back to health, "'He might as well plant an oak in a flowerpot, and expect it to thrive, as imagine he can restore her to vigor in the soil of his shallow cares.'" Explain how this **metaphor** relates to the wider **symbolism** of Nature in the novel.
43. Explain what Lockwood means by his reference to Catherine Heathcliff in the final paragraph of the chapter.

Chapters Fifteen & Sixteen

44. In these chapters there are several instances of **foreshadowing**. [Think of Cathy at Lockwood's window!] Find and comment on two.
45. Analyze the **symbolism** of the description of Cathy's grave which ends Ch.16.

Chapter Seventeen

46. Isabella's action in escaping Wuthering Heights shows a strength of will of which she has previously seemed incapable. How does the writer explain this change in her character?
47. Mrs. Dean says of Edgar, "*He* didn't pray for Catherine's soul to haunt him." Contrast the reactions of Heathcliff and Edgar to the death of Cathy.
48. What does Heathcliff mean when he says that Hindley's body "'should be buried at the cross-roads, without ceremony of any kind'"? What light does Joseph's statement immediately afterwards to the doctor throw on Hindley's death?

Chapters Eighteen & Nineteen

Isabella's death occurs in the summer of 1797 (Foerster, 27).

49. What features of young Cathy's character clearly derive from each of her parents?
50. Compare Cathy's initial reactions to Hareton and to Linton. Explain how Cathy denies her true nature in preferring Linton over Hareton. How does this error recall her mother's choices?

Chapters Twenty & Twenty-one

51. Heathcliff says of Linton, "'he's *mine*, and I want the triumph of seeing *my* descendant fairly lord of their estates: my child hiring their children…'" Explain briefly, but clearly, how Heathcliff plans to accomplish this end.
52. Describing Cathy as she was before she met Linton at Wuthering Heights, Mrs. Dean says, "She was a happy creature, and an angel, in those days. It's a pity she could not be content." Explain exactly why it is psychologically impossible for Cathy to be content. What does Mrs. Dean's statement **foreshadow**?
53. Seeing Hareton with Cathy, Heathcliff comments, "'I know what he suffers now, for instance, exactly; it is merely a beginning of what he shall suffer though.'" Explain Heathcliff's **motivation** for his treatment of Hareton.
54. Comment on the **extended metaphor** which Mrs. Dean uses to describe Cathy's reaction to the discovery of the loss of her letters from Linton, "Never did any bird flying back to a plundered nest… express more complete despair… than she."

Chapters Twenty-two & Twenty-three

55. Analyze the **symbolism** of Mrs. Dean's description of the "little flower up yonder" and of stretching on top of the wall to reach fruit. [Do not neglect Cathy's statement near the end of this section, "'I can get over the wall.'"]

Chapter Twenty-four

56. Linton and Cathy argue about "'the pleasantest manner of spending a hot July day.'" What does the reader learn about the differences in their characters from what each says?
57. How does Mrs. Dean make it clear in her **narrative** that Cathy sadly misjudges the respective natures of Linton and Hareton? What is the basis of her bias in this matter?
58. What is **foreshadowed** by the final sentence of chapter twenty-four?

Chapters Twenty-five & Twenty-six

Mrs. Dean tells Lockwood that these events happened last winter, that is, the winter of 1800-1801. Nelly's three-week illness supposedly occurs in November 1800, but she also states that it occurs in February 1801. Cathy's seventeenth birthday is on March 20th, 1801. She was born, of course, on the day her mother died, a date which the writer chose carefully because it is the vernal equinox, the point of the year when dark and light, death and life, are in equal balance, as winter yields to the renewal of spring (Foerster, 33).

59. Explain the full significance of Edgar's comment to Mrs. Dean that he will not visit his wife's grave on the anniversary of her death as is his custom but will "'defer it this year a little longer.'"
60. What are the factors that account for Linton's "'curious **mood**'" when he meets Cathy and Mrs. Dean by agreement on the moor.

Chapters Twenty-seven & Twenty-eight

Cathy's escape from Wuthering Heights occurs at the harvest moon near the autumnal equinox when summer ripens into the promise of fruition. Edgar's death occurs in September 1801, two months before Lockwood's first visit to Wuthering Heights (Foerster, 33).

61. How does Brontë (through the **narrative** of Mrs. Dean) seek to make believable Edgar's approval of the idea that Cathy should marry Linton? How successful do you find the explanation?

62. Explain Heathcliff's **motivation** in seeking the marriage of Cathy and Linton. Some critics have claimed that Heathcliff's unyielding desire for revenge makes him not only inhuman but diabolical and therefore an unbelievable character. What do you think? Support your conclusion with two detailed references to the text.

Chapter Twenty-nine

63. In this chapter, both the **frame narrative** and Heathcliff's own story have almost come full circle. Explain. [Incidentally, it should now be perfectly clear to you who Cathy will marry at the end of the novel and why.]

64. Heathcliff's descriptions of his behavior at Catherine's grave both on the night of her burial and at the burial beside her of Edgar are shocking. Why do you think that the writer includes them? [The **genre** term **Gothic** is important to a full understanding of this novel.]

Chapter Thirty & Thirty-one

65. In these chapters we see the re-emergence of Hareton's noble nature. (In truth, there have been hints of its survival throughout the **narrative**, but you have to look very carefully to find them.) Trace the stages of his attempts to make himself agreeable to Cathy, and comment on her reaction to his behavior.

66. If you put together something that Zillah says about Cathy's resistance to Heathcliff, and something that Lockwood himself notices about Heathcliff when he meets him at Wuthering Heights, you should be able to conclude something about the dynamic of the relationship between Heathcliff and Cathy at this time.

Chapter Thirty-two & Thirty-three

The opening of Chapter Thirty-two may be a little obscure. Lockwood has been invited by his friend to go grouse hunting on his moors. The grouse season opens in August.

67. Why was it inevitable all along that Cathy and Hareton would fall in love? How does their love resolve the conflicts in Catherine's **tragic** love affair with Heathcliff? [These are actually the same question.] Remember Lockwood's own failed love affair. See the links?

68. In the incident where Heathcliff attacks Cathy and seems "ready to tear Catherine to pieces," explain why you think that he suddenly desists.
69. Nelly says of Cathy and Hareton "their eyes are precisely similar, and they are those of Catherine Earnshaw." What does this statement add to the reader's understanding of the unlikely love of Cathy and Hareton?
70. Account for Heathcliff's sudden change. Why does he feel "'I am surrounded with her [Catherine's] **image**'"? What is it that he is convinced "'will be reached – and soon – because it has devoured my existence'"?

Chapter Thirty-four

71. What is significant about Heathcliff's choice of bedchamber on the last night of his life? How does Mrs. Dean misinterpret his **motivation**? [What has the window come to **symbolize** in the novel?]
72. Contrast Mrs. Dean's rational description of finding Heathcliff's dead body and her explanation of what happened with what the reader might conclude about the 'true' circumstances of Heathcliff's death.
73. How does the writer maintain to the end of the novel **ambiguity** concerning the fate of Cathy and Heathcliff after their deaths?

Works Cited:

Foerster, Richard. *Novel Study Guide "Wuthering Heights" by Emily Brontë.* first edition. Austin: Holt, Rinehart and Winston.

Phillips, Brian and Bourneuf, Annie. *SparkNote on Wuthering Heights.* 13 May. 2006 <http://www.sparknotes.com/lit/wuthering/>.

Wasowski, Richard P. *CliffsNotes on Wuthering Heights.* 24 Jul 2006 <http://www.cliffsnotes.com/WileyCDA/LitNote/id-164.html>.

Further Reading:

"Wuthering Heights" by Sylvia Plath and "Wuthering Heights" by Ted Hughes. The husband and wife poets visited the ruins of Wuthering Heights together but produced very different poems.

Activity: Character map

Create a character map to show how Heathcliff affects or is affected by each of the following characters:
Edgar, Isabella (Edgar's sister), Catherine, Hindley (Catherine's brother), Cathy (Edgar and Catherine's daughter), Linton (Heathcliff and Isabella's son), Hareton (Hindley's son)

Activity: Literary Terms

As you use each term in the study guide, fill in the definition of the term and include an example from the text to show how it is used.

The first definition is supplied. Find an example in the text to complete it.

Term	Definition
	Example
ambiguous, ambiguity	*when a statement is unclear in meaning- ambiguity may be deliberate or accidental*
analogy	
diction	
foreshadow	
frame narrative	

A Study Guide

Term	Definition / Example
genre	
image	
irony	
irony, verbal	
melodramatic	
metaphor	

Term	Definition
	Example
metaphor, extended	
mood	
motivation	
narrative	
narrator	
paradox	

Term	Definition
	Example
perspective	
setting	
simile	
symbol, symbolic, symbolism, symbolize	
tone	
tragic	

Wuthering Heights by Emily Brontë

Literary terms

NOTE Not all of these terms may be relevant to this particular study guide

Allegorical: a story in which the characters, their actions and the settings represent abstract ideas (often moral ideas) or historical/ political events.

Ambiguous, ambiguity: when a statement is unclear in meaning- ambiguity may be deliberate or accidental

Analogy: a comparison which treats two things as identical in one or more specified ways

Antagonist: an opposing character or force to the protagonist

Antithesis: the complete opposite of something

Authorial comment: when the writer addresses the reader directly (not to be confused with the narrator doing so.)

Climax: the conflict to which the action has been building since the start of the play or story.

Colloquialism: the casual, informal mainly spoken language of ordinary people - often called" slang".

Comic hyperbole: deliberately inflated, extravagant language used for comic effect

Connotation: the ideas, feelings and associations generated by a word or phrase

Dark comedy: comedy which has a serious implication

Dialogue: a conversation between two or more people in direct speech

Diction: the writer's choice of words in order to create a particular effect

Dramatic function or purpose: some characters and plot devices in plays are used by the author for specific purposes necessary to the action

Equivocation: saying something which is capable of two interpretations with the intention of misrepresenting the truth

Euphemism: a polite word for an ugly truth for example, a person is said to be sleeping when they are actually dead

Fallacy: a misconception resulting from incorrect reasoning

Foreshadow: a statement or action which gives the reader a hint of what is likely to happen later in the narrative

Form of speech: the register in which speech is written - the diction reflects the character

Frame narrative: a story within which the main narrative is placed

Genre: the type of literature into which a particular text falls (e.g. drama, poetry, novel)

Hyperbole: exaggeration designed to create a particular effect

Image, imagery: figurative language such as simile, metaphor, personification etc., or a description which conjures u a particularly vivid picture

Imply, implication: when the text suggests to the reader a meaning which it does not actually state

Infer, inference: the reader's act of going beyond what is stated in the text to draw conclusions

Irony, ironic: a form of humor which undercuts the apparent meaning of a statement

> *Conscious irony:* irony used deliberately by a writer or character
>
> *Unconscious irony:* a statement or action which has significance for the reader of which the character is unaware
>
> *Dramatic irony:* when an action has an important significance that is obvious to the reader but not to one or more of the characters
>
> *Tragic irony:* when a character says (or does) something which will have a serious, even fatal, consequence for him/ her. The audience is aware of the error, but the character is not.
>
> *Verbal irony:* the conscious use of particular words which are appropriate to what is being said

Juxtaposition: literally putting two things side by side for purposes of comparison and/ or contrast

Literal: the surface level of a statement

Machiavellian: a person for whom the end justifies the means - a devious, manipulative, character whose only concern is his/ her own good

Melodramatic: action and/or dialogue that is inflated or extravagant- frequently used for comic effect

Metaphor, metaphorical: the description of one thing by direct comparison with another (e.g. the coal-black night)

> *Extended metaphor: a comparison which is developed at length*

Microcosm: literally 'the world is little' - a situation which reflects truths about the world in general

Mood: the feelings and emotions contained in and/ or produced by a work of art (text, painting, music, etc.)

Motif: a frequently repeated idea, image or situation

Motivation: why a character acts as he/ she does- in modern literature motivation is seen as psychological

Narrates, narrator: the voice that the reader hears in the text

> *Frame narrative /story:* a story within which the main story is told (e.g. "heart of darkness" by Conrad begins with five men on a boat in the Thames and then one of them tells the story of his experiences on the river Congo)

Oxymoron: the juxtaposition of two terms normally thought of as opposite (e.g. the silent scream)

Parable: a story with a moral lesson (e.g. the Good Samaritan)

Paradox, paradoxical: a statement or situation which appears self-contradictory and therefore absurd

Pathos: is pity, or rather the ability of a text to make the audience or reader feel pity

Perspective: point of view from which a story, or an incident within a story, is told

Personified, personification: a simile or metaphor in which an inanimate object or abstract idea is described by comparison with a human

Plot: a chain of events linked by cause and effect

Prologue: an introduction which gives a lead-in to the main story

Protagonist: the character who initiates the action and is most likely to have the sympathy of the audience

Realism: a text that describes the action in a way that appears to reflect life

Rhetoric: the art of public speaking and more specifically the techniques which make speaking and writing effective

Rhetorical device: any use of language designed to make the expression of ideas more effective (e.g. repetition, imagery, alliteration, etc.)

Role: means function- characters in plays (particularly minor characters) frequently have specific functions

Sarcasm: stronger than irony - it involves a deliberate attack on a person or idea with the intention of mocking

Satire, Satiric; the use of comedy to criticize attack, belittle, or humiliate- more extreme than irony

Setting: the environment in which the narrative (or part of the narrative) takes place

Simile: a description of one thing by explicit comparison with another (e.g. my love is like a red, red rose)

> *Extended simile*: a comparison which is developed at length

Stoicism, stoic: This is taking everything which life throws at you very calmly. Stoics thought you should judge a person by how they behaved rather than what they said.

Style: the way in which a writer chooses to express him/ herself. Style is a vital aspect of meaning since how something is expressed can crucially affect what is being written or spoken

Suspense: the building of tension in the reader

Symbol, symbolic, symbolism, symbolize: a physical object which comes to represent an abstract idea (e.g. the sun may symbolize life)

Themes: important concepts, beliefs and ideas explored and presented in a text

Tone: literally the sound of a text - How words sound (either in the mouth of an actor or the head of a reader) can crucially affect meaning

Tragic: King Richard III and Macbeth are both murderous tyrants, yet only Macbeth is a *tragic* figure. Why? Because Macbeth has the potential to be great, recognizes the error he has made and all that he has lost in making it, and dies bravely in a way that seems to accept the justice of the punishment.

Graphic #1 Plot Graph for *Wuthering Heights*

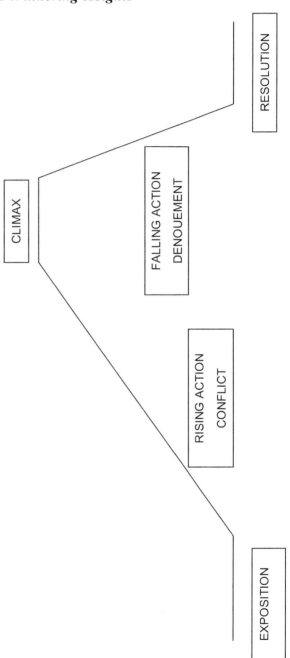

Plot graph for *Wuthering Heights*

CLIMAX

RESOLUTION

FALLING ACTION
DENOUEMENT

RISING ACTION
CONFLICT

EXPOSITION

Graphic #2 Different perspectives on the situation which initiates the action in the novel

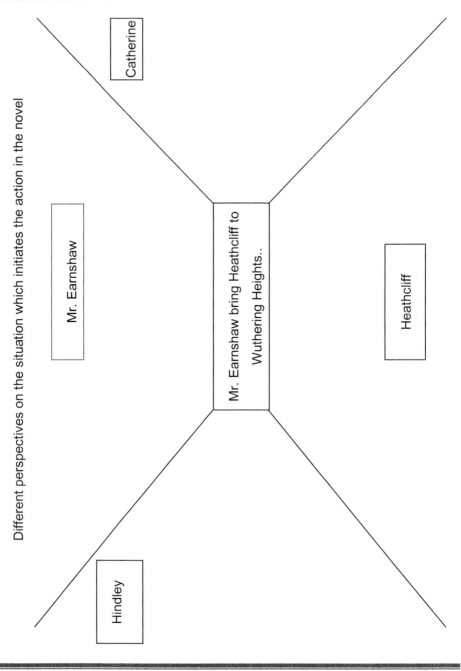

To the Reader,

I strive to make my products the best that they can be. If you have any comments or question about this book *please* contact the author through his email: **moore.ray1@yahoo.com**

Visit my website at **http://www.raymooreauthor.com**

Also by Ray Moore:

All books are available from amazon.com and from barnesandnoble.com as paperbacks and at most online eBook retailers.

Fiction:

The Lyle Thorne Mysteries: each book features five tales from the Golden Age of Detection:

> *Investigations of The Reverend Lyle*
> *Further Investigations of The Reverend Lyle Thorne*
> *Early Investigations of Lyle Thorne*
> *Sanditon Investigations of The Reverend Lyle Thorne*

Non-fiction:- listed alphabetically by author

The ***Critical Introduction series*** is written for high school teachers and students and for college undergraduates. Each volume gives an in-depth analysis of a key text:

> *"Pride and Prejudice" by Jane Austen: A Critical Introduction*
> *"The Stranger" by Albert Camus: A Critical Introduction*
> *"The General Prologue" by Geoffrey Chaucer: A Critical Introduction*
> *"The Great Gatsby" by F. Scott Fitzgerald: A Critical Introduction*

The Text and Critical Introduction series differs from the Critical introduction series as these books contain the original medieval text together with an interlinear translation to aid the understanding of the text. The commentary allows the reader to develop a deeper understanding of the text and themes within the text.

> *"The Wife of Bath's Prologue and Tale" by Geoffrey Chaucer: Text and Critical Introduction*
> *"Sir Gawain and the Green Knight": Text and Critical Introduction*
> *"The General Prologue" by Geoffrey Chaucer: Text and Critical Introduction*

Other Study Guides available as e-books:

"Jane Eyre" by Charlotte Brontë: A Study Guide

"Wuthering Heights" by Emily Brontë: A Study Guide

"The Myth of Sisyphus" and "The Stranger" by Albert Camus: Two Study Guides

"Heart of Darkness" by Joseph Conrad: A Study Guide

"Great Expectations" by Charles Dickens: A Study Guide

"The Mill on the Floss" by George Eliot: A Study Guide

"Catch-22" by Joseph Heller: A Study Guide

"Nineteen Eighty-Four by George Orwell: A Study Guide

"Selected Poems" by Sylvia Plath: A Study Guide

"Henry IV Part 2" by William Shakespeare: A Study Guide

"Julius Caesar" by William Shakespeare: A Study Guide

"Macbeth" by William Shakespeare: A Study Guide

"Of Mice and Men" by John Steinbeck: A Study Guide

"The Pearl" by John Steinbeck: A Study Guide

"Slaughterhouse-Five" by Kurt Vonnegut: A Study Guide

"The Bridge of San Luis Rey" by Thornton Wilder: A Study Guide

Teacher resources:

Ray also publishes many more study guides and other resources for classroom use on the 'Teacher Pay Teachers' website:

http://www.teacherspayteachers.com/Store/Raymond-Moore

Printed in Great Britain
by Amazon